THE HISTORY OF THE

The Pug's origins can be traced back to ancient China. Perhaps because of the ancient nature of the Pug, his origins are shrouded in mystery. We do know that accounts of Pug-like dogs dating back as far as 1000 BC have been found, though we do not know where these early Pugs came from. It seems the Pug is as close to an original breed as possible.

The Pug was a favorite of royalty in ancient China, an affection that seems to have persisted through the last dynasty. There are accounts of Pugs being favored by members of the royal family and being given as gifts to visiting diplomats.

The ancient beginnings of the Pug make him as close to an original breed as possible.

THE PUG IN EUROPE

How this breed made its way to Europe is also somewhat obscure. The sailors who imported the breed from China did not keep records of their canine cargo. We don't how how far the Pug was spread across the European continent or how common it was.

The Pug might well have arrived first in Holland, brought by Dutch sailors from expeditions to the East. We do know that Holland was the first country in which the Pug rose to popularity.

Pugs had always been a favorite pet in the Dutch ruling house, but they gained a special status after a Pug saved the life of William the Silent, Duke of Orange. Spanish troops attacked the duke's camp in the middle of the night. The duke's Pug, Pompey, woke his master upon hearing something strange, and the duke narrowly escaped the ambush. When William came from Holland in the late 1600s to assume the throne of Great Britain, he brought a host of Pugs with orange ribbons tied around their necks as part of his entourage.

This royal endorsement must have done much to increase Pugs' popularity in England, for the English seem to have taken to Pugs with a similar fervor. Pugs are depicted in the 18th century etchings of William Hogarth. They are also present in paintings of various members of the English royal family through the nineteenth century. Pugs were one of Queen Victoria's favorite breeds.

THE BLACK PUG

Queen Victoria herself owned a black Pug, but during this era and before the overall feeling about them was negative. They were typically culled from litters and generally considered inferior.

But this sentiment was about to be radically changed. The popularity of the black Pug can be traced to a single woman, and it was not Queen Victoria. In 1876, while in China, Lady Brassey acquired several black Pugs. She brought them back to England and proudly exhibited them at a dog show there. They became an instant hit. Now, although fawn Pugs outnumber blacks by almost ten to one, they are in no way considered inferior specimens. In fact, several kennels today specialize in black Pugs.

THE PUG IN AMERICA

When the first Pug arrived in the United States is a matter of speculation, but we do know that

Many 18th century etchings and paintings depict the Pug.

The black Pug did not become popular until the late 1800s. Although fawn Pugs outnumber blacks today, many kennels specialize in breeding black Pugs.

several of them were exhibited in 1879 in New York. Early American breeders acquired most of their stock from England, but many also imported Pugs from China to revitalize and strengthen the breed. This practice of importing Chinese Pugs was simultaneously happening in England, so the Pug breed on both sides of the Atlantic was infused with fresh blood.

In 1885, Pugs were accepted by the American Kennel Club and and the first American standard for the Pug was written and approved. This standard has been touched up a few times since then, but the original standard remains largely intact, yet another testament to this enduring breed.

During the early decades of the twentieth century, Pugs' popularity took a back seat to other Toy breeds like the Pekingese and the Pomeranian. By 1931, however, the breed's popularity was on an upsurge again and the Pug Dog Club of America was formed. Since the 1950s especially the Pug has been steadily increasing in popularity.

Today the Pug is one of the most popular breeds in the country. From its earliest origins in ancient China to the present day it has been bred as a companion animal. As a result of thousands of years of perfecting the breed, the Pug today is a companion like no other dog. He

One theory of how the Pug got his name suggests that it comes from the word *pugnus*, the Latin word for fist, because the Pug's face looks like a closed fist.

has been bred to excel at this and has proved his exceptional ability throughout history.

THE NAME PUG

Where does the name Pug come from? No, it's not short for anything, and like the little dog itself it stands on its own. There are a few theories about how this breed came to me called "Pug." In the eighteenth century, pug was a nickname for a pet monkey or dog. In time this epithet became reserved for one breed of dog in particular, a favorite with the ladies of the aristocracy. Another theory holds that the name Pug refers to the Latin word for fist, *pugnus*, because the Pug's face looks like a closed fist. We'll never know for certain just how this little dog got its name, but everyone agrees that this short, powerful word perfectly suits the short yet impressive Pug.

FAMOUS PUGS

Pugs were the favorite dogs of the Duke and Duchess of Windsor. In fact, on his deathbed the Duke was comforted by his favorite Pug, Diamond. Queen Victoria loved her Pugs and was greatly responsible for their increased popularity. As a favorite companion of the upper classes, the Pug is commonly pictured in eighteenth and nineteenth century art from William Hogarth to Tissot.

DESCRIPTION OF THE BREED

What is it about Pugs that attracts people to them? It is no doubt their charming looks, their small manageable size and their ease of care. It is also their friendly personality and affectionate nature. Indeed, there are many irresistible things about the Pug, but before you commit to bring any animal into your life you must decide if you can accommodate its particular needs. Before you buy a dog, do some research into the specific needs of your chosen breed. If you already have a Pug, it's never too late to learn a little more to make your relationship even better.

The Pug's motto is *Mealtime in Parve,* which means, basically, that the Pug is a lot of dog in a small package. This is a perfect description of this little dog, for although he is a Toy, he is no delicate flower. He is a square, muscular dog that gives the impression of strength.

The Pug is the dog for all occasions: He is small enough to be a lap dog yet sturdy enough to

Wherever you go, your Pug wants to be right there with you—even on vacation!

accompany his family on long walks in the country. He belongs in the Toy Group not because he is a diminutive of a larger breed, but because his main purpose is and always has been to be a companion.

TEMPERAMENT

The Pug is a social dog; while he will certainly become attached to his main caretaker (namely the person who puts down the food dish) he is not a one-person dog and will befriend equally all the people in his family.

He likes to be where the action is. He will walk with you outdoors or sit with you quietly as you read a book. He will want to be a part of what you are doing at all times, for his greatest pleasure in life is being with you.

Pugs and children are a natural combination. Your Pug will be a playful and patient companion for children who know how to treat him well. He is sturdy enough to participate in all their games and can be an equally valuable companion in quieter hours. Make sure you teach your children from the outset that they must treat your Pug with respect and care; he is a dog not a toy.

Pugs also get along well with other dogs. Other dogs, however, may not be as friendly and non-territorial as Pugs tend to be. If you are introducing a new Pug into a house with another dog who may have a problem accepting the newcomer, introduce them in a neutral environment.

Pugs and children make a perfect combination. Make sure children are taught to treat their pet with lots of love and respect.

Pugs get along well with other dogs if the introductions are made properly. This group of Pugs rush to meet the new guys on the block.

Many owners are tempted to get two Pugs...or three...or four...or more!

Many Pug owners find that the perfect companion for their Pug is another Pug. However, if you think you want two Pugs, do not be tempted to get two puppies at the same time. Two puppies may bond with each other before they bond with you. You want to make sure you have the opportunity to form a special relationship with each dog, so wait a year or so after buying your first Pug to acquire your second.

The Pug is not a yappy dog like some other Toy breeds, though he will certainly bark as a stranger approaches the door. Although his small size prevents him from being a real watch dog, his warning will certainly deter trespassers.

APPEARANCE

The Pug's head is one of its most important features. The head is large and round, and impressive. The Pug is a brachycephalic (short-nosed) breed. The wrinkles on the Pug's face around the eyes and nose contribute, along with its round deep brown eyes, to the Pug's characteristic expression. Its face, with it's black nose and muzzle and wide eager eyes, is a great part of its charm.

The Pug's body is compact, square, and well-muscled. He is a strong, sturdy dog who is small in size, though not in presence. The tail curled up over the back completes the image of an alert, playful pet.

Pugs need plenty of fresh air and exercise. Otis and Samson owned by Lori Visceglia love spending time outdoors.

The Pug owes a great part of his charm to his face, with its black nose and muzzle, wrinkles, and wide eager eyes.

LIFE SPAN

A well-cared for Pug will live on average from twelve to fifteen years. The chin and muzzle of most Pugs will start greying when they are still quite young, anywhere from two to six years of age.

PUG QUIRKS

For all his eagerness to get along with his family, the Pug still has a great deal of personality. Pugs can be very stubborn. They like routine and are quite likely to resent a change in their normal activities, though with urging they will come around eventually.

EXERCISE REQUIREMENTS

One thing Pugs hate is to be put on a diet, for to a Pug food is the greatest pleasure in life after being with his family. You must be careful to monitor your Pug's diet, as he will generally eat whatever is in front of him and then go looking for more. For this reason, Pugs with indulgent owners can easily become obese, a condition that is not only unattractive but extremely unhealthy.

You must be sure to offer your Pug plenty of exercise. Pugs are, like many people, prone to be couch potatoes. They are not wildly energetic dogs who need to run around in the park for two hours before they calm down. This means that setting up a sensible exercise routine for your Pug is all the more your responsibility. A possible routine might include a quick paced mile walk in the morning, another before dinner, and a romp in the afternoon.

Also, consider getting involved in organized activities with your Pug. Obedience training and agility work are challenging ways to keep active with your Pug. Both you and your Pug will benefit from obedience training, which will teach your Pug basic manners and skills, stimulate his mind and keep him active; working together will both deepen your bond and help you understand how your Pug's mind works. In addition, attending obedience classes will socialize your Pug.

Although Pugs are known to have a stubborn streak, many have proven themselves in the fields of agility and obedience competition. These activities will improve your relationship with your dog and give him a chance to succeed at a challenging task.

A note of caution: because Pugs are short nosed you must be careful not to exercise them in the extreme heat as they can become overheated quickly. Set exercise times in the early morning and late afternoon during the hottest times of the year.

Consider getting your Pug involved in organized activities such as obedience training and conformation showing. Both you and your Pug will benefit from it.

PUG NOISES

Another characteristic attributable to the Pug's shortened muzzle is that Pugs have a tendency to make noise. They may grunt or snort, although experienced pug owners consider these noises attempts at verbal communication. In addition, many Pugs snore. Most pug owners find this noise charming!

PUG STANDARD

General Appearance— Symmetry and general appearance are decidedly square and cobby. A lean, leggy Pug and a dog with short legs and a long body are equally objectionable.

Size, Proportion, Substance— The Pug should be *multum in parvo,* and this condensation (if the word may be used) is shown by compactness of form, well knit proportions, and hardness of developed muscle. Weight from 14 to 18 pounds (dog or bitch) desirable. *Proportion* square.

Head—The *head* is large, massive, round-not apple-headed, with no indentation of the *skull.* The *eyes* are dark in color, very large, bold and prominent, globular in shape, soft and solicitous in *expression,* very lustrous, and, when excited, full of fire. The *ears* are thin, small, soft, like black velvet. There are two kinds—the "rose" and the "button." Preference is given to the latter. The *wrinkles* are large and deep. The *muzzle* is short, blunt, square, but not upfaced. A Pug's *bite* should be very slightly undershot.

Neck, Topline, Body—The *neck* is slightly arched. It is strong, thick, and with enough length to carry the head proudly. The short *back* is level from the withers to the high tail set. The *body* is short and cobby, wide in chest and well ribbed up. The *tail* is curled as tightly as possible over the hip. The double curl is perfection.

Forequarters—The *legs* are very strong, straight, of moderate length, and are set well under. The *elbows* should be directly under the withers when viewed from the side. The shoulders are moderately laid back. The *pasterns* are strong, neither steep nor down. The *feet* are neither so long as the foot of the hare, nor so round as that of the cat; well split-up toes, and the nails black. Dewclaws are generally removed.

Hindquarters—The strong, powerful hindquarters have moderate bend of *stifle* and short *hocks* perpendicular to the ground. The *legs* are parallel when viewed from behind. The hindquarters are in balance with the forequarters. The *thighs* and *buttocks* are full and muscular. *Feet* as in front.

Coat—The coat is fine, smooth, soft, short and glossy, neither hard nor woolly.

Color—The colors are silver, apricot-fawn, or black. The silver or apricot-fawn colors should be decided so as to make the contrast complete between the color and the trace and the mask.

Markings —The *markings* are clearly defined. The muzzle or mask, ears, moles on cheeks, thumb mark or diamond on forehead, and the back trace should be as black as possible. The mask should be black. The more intense and well defined it is, the better. The trace is a black line extending from the occiput to the tail.

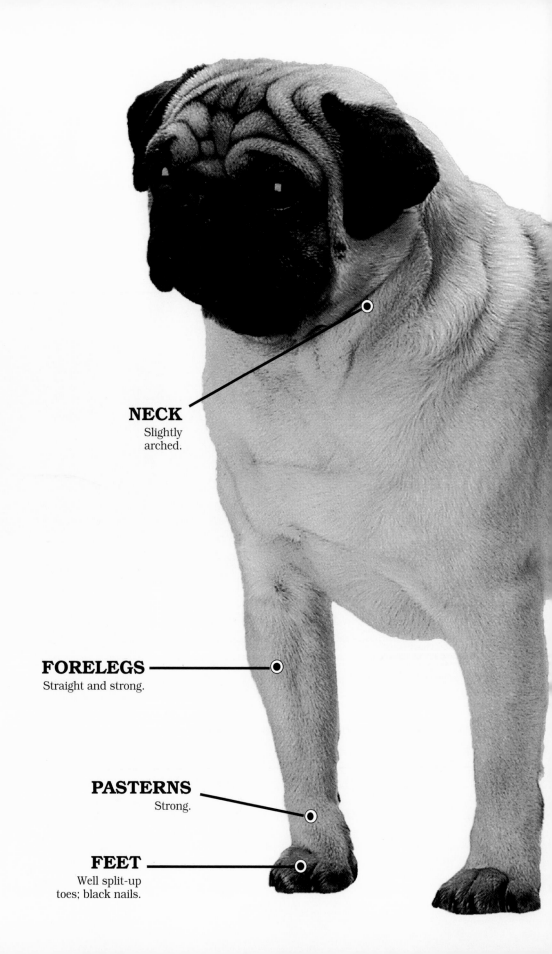

NECK
Slightly arched.

FORELEGS
Straight and strong.

PASTERNS
Strong.

FEET
Well split-up toes; black nails.

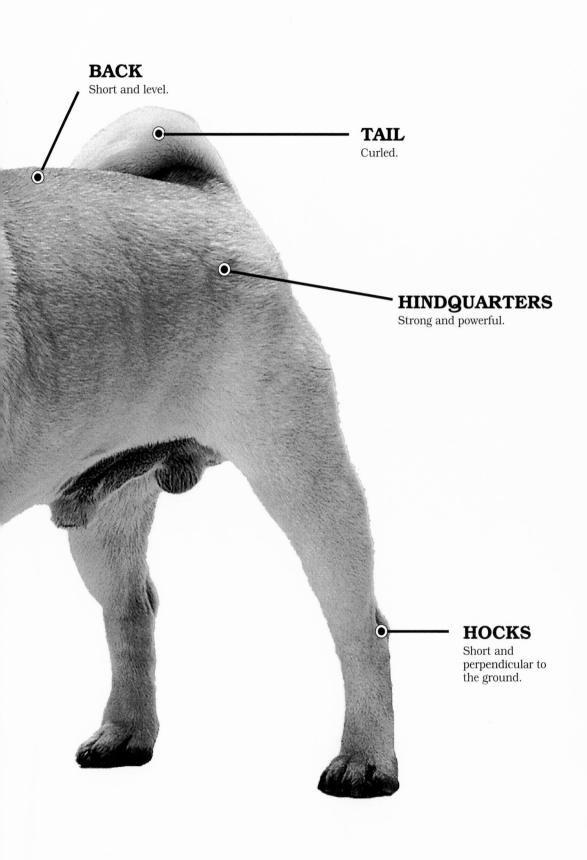

BACK
Short and level.

TAIL
Curled.

HINDQUARTERS
Strong and powerful.

HOCKS
Short and
perpendicular to
the ground.

Even as puppies, Pugs exhibit playfulness and an outgoing disposition.

A Pug's greatest pleasure is pleasing his owner. His main purpose is and always has been as a companion.

Gait—Viewed from the front, the forelegs should be carried well forward, showing no weakness in the pasterns, the paws landing squarely with the central toes straight ahead. The rear action should be strong and free through hocks and stifles, with no twisting or turning in or out at the joints. The hind legs should follow in line with the front. There is a slight natural convergence of the limbs both fore and aft. A slight roll of the hindquarters typifies the gait which should be free, self-assured, and jaunty.

Temperament—This is an even-tempered breed, exhibiting stability, playfulness, great charm, dignity, and an outgoing, loving disposition.

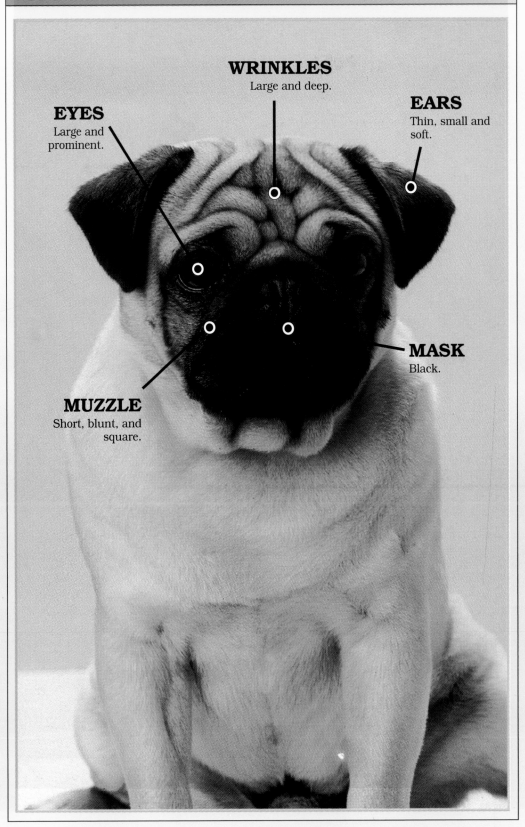

WRINKLES
Large and deep.

EARS
Thin, small and soft.

EYES
Large and prominent.

MASK
Black.

MUZZLE
Short, blunt, and square.

Choose a Pug puppy who is bright-eyed and alert.

YOUR NEW PUG PUPPY

In your excitement to have your own Pug, don't just choose the first puppy you see, do some research beforehand. You will be sharing over a decade of your life with this companion, so make sure your Pug is the right one from the very beginning. Reading this section is a good start.

When you go to look at puppies, it is often hard to choose just one. They are so cute, you want to take them all home! But there are a few things to keep in mind that will make finding a Pug for you an easier task. Choose a puppy that is bright-eyed and alert, with no signs of illness like a runny nose or watery eyes. Resist the temptation to choose the Pug who lingers in the corner, the quiet one who seems to be the runt. This kind of behavior could just mean the puppy is a late bloomer, in which case he isn't ready to leave home yet; worse, it could indicate a serious illness or personality problem. You want to have the healthiest, happiest Pug you can right from the start. If possible, let your Pug choose you. The eager youngster who saunters

You should accustom your Pug puppy to wearing his collar and identification tags as soon as you get him home.

right up to you for a closer look and some friendly attention is probably the one.

When you purchase your purebred Pug you will have a little paperwork to go over with the breeder or previous owner. The papers should include information about ownership, registration and health-related information, such as vaccinations and wormings. Also ask for a meal's worth of the food the puppy has been eating and his feeding schedule. If possible, try to get this information ahead of time so you can have a supply on hand when your new puppy arrives home.

There are other things you will need to do to prepare for your Pug's arrival. The first step is to have a veterinarian. (See the health chapter for more information on choosing a veterinarian.) Make sure you do this before you bring your puppy home. You will need to take the puppy to the vet within a few days of bringing him home for a thorough check-up, and that is not the time to try to find a good veterinarian.

You will also need a few supplies: a crate and some soft bedding, food and water dishes, a Nylabone® dog chew, and a supply of the food he was being fed in his previous home. Try to have these on hand before you bring your puppy home so you can settle straight into enjoying him without having to run to the store.

These Pug puppies are too young to go to their new homes. You must wait until puppies are at least eight weeks old.

You will need to have toys ready for your puppy's arrival. Gumabones® are great for teething puppies due to their softer composition.

When you bring your puppy home, let him wander around and explore his new surroundings, although you might find that after a brief excursion he lies down for a long nap. The experience of moving to a new place with new people is an exciting and stressful thing for your puppy, so it is very important to let him have as much sleep as he needs and take his time adjusting.

Keep visitors and occasions to a minimum the first few days. Although all the neighborhood children will be keen to see your new Pug, ask them to wait a few days before visiting. Let your Pug become secure in his relationship with you before he is exposed to a whole new set of people. Pugs and children will become great friends, but this can only happen if boundaries are respected. Make sure the children know that the dog is not a plaything and should not be treated as such. Children can learn the proper way to carry a puppy, but with a group of children, it's probably better to ask that they leave the puppy on the floor at all times. Most importantly, always supervise your puppy with your children until you are totally secure in their behavior.

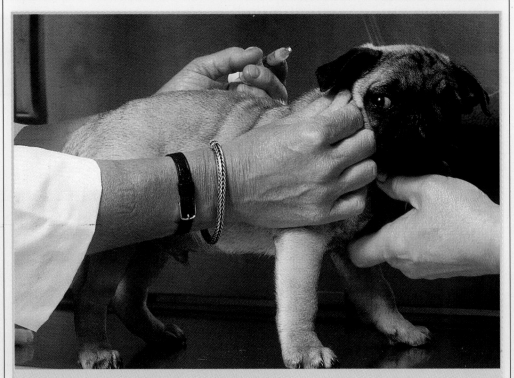

Although your puppy should have at least one set of inoculations when you bring him home, it is up to you to keep his vaccinations up-to-date.

THE FIRST NIGHT

The first night your Pug is home with you, he will probably be scared and whiny. Imagine being separated from everything familiar. It's wonderful for a while, but when you're alone in the dark you will be quite ready to say let's go home now! Once you understand that, you realize you must never get angry with your Pug if he cries during the night. Handle the situation correctly, and soon he will be over it for good.

You have purchased a crate and made it comfortable with soft bedding, maybe an old towel or blanket. Throw in a piece of your clothing; this smells like you and will be reassuring to your Pug as he falls asleep.

When it is bedtime, put your Pug in his comfy crate and put the crate next to your bed. This way he'll soon learn the crate is his bed, and he'll be comforted by your close presence. When he starts to cry, put your hand on the crate to comfort him, but don't take him out. Some people also recommend placing a radio turned down very low next to his crate or wrapping a ticking alarm clock in a towel and placing this inside the crate. This supposedly simulates the mother's heartbeat and calms the puppy.

After a week or so, move the crate to the place you have established as the puppy's sleeping quarters, somewhere fairly out of the way so the puppy can retreat to his crate during the

Your Pug should always view his crate as a safe and secure haven—and a place to store all of his Nylabone® toys!

day if he feels the need for some privacy. Put the puppy to bed in his crate, which he has now come to identify as a safe and secure haven. Doing it this way will give your puppy independence and build confidence step by step, rather than in one brutal swoop.

HOUSEBREAKING

This is a challenge you will be facing from the very beginning, but with consistency and patience, housetraining your Pug will be no problem. To paper train your Pug, just establish a bathroom corner somewhere in the house. When he urinates, wipe it up and blot a bit of it on a piece of newspaper. Put this newspaper on top of a fairly thick layer in the predetermined bathroom corner, and show him where it is. When he has to urinate again, he will seek out the bathroom corner. When you clean it up, leave a bit of urine on the top newspapers so he will know where to go again.

To housetrain him, transfer this routine to your yard. Make sure you take the puppy outside when he wakes up, after he has eaten every meal, before he goes to bed and many times in between. Seek out the same bathroom spot every time and he will soon be used to the new routine. You will have to pick up the papers or he will just go back to the easy way.

Ask the breeder what kind of food the puppy has been eating and for a feeding schedule. Try to get this information ahead of time so that you can have a supply on hand when your puppy comes home.

FEEDING YOUR PUG

Providing your Pug with a healthy diet is one of the most important things you will do to keep him healthy and in prime condition. The good news is it's also one of the easiest, though many people will tell you otherwise.

NUTRITIONAL NEEDS

Your Pug has basic nutritional needs, though these will change somewhat throughout his life. As a puppy, he will need lots of protein in his diet to develop healthy bones and tissues. As he ages, an excess of protein is unnecessary and can be unhealthy. When your Pug is a senior citizen, he may need a "diet" food that is low in protein and calories.

So what's the easiest way to satisfy your Pug's nutritional needs? People have many different opinions about that, many people have secret formulas they swear by or different routines that they follow assiduously. But feeding your Pug correctly doesn't need to be a complicated thing.

Researchers at major dog food companies spend thousands of dollars and hours determining the

For their first weeks of life, Pug puppies receive the nutrition they need from their mother.

correct amount of different elements for dogs in various stages. Take advantage of all this effort. By far the easiest and most nutritionally balanced food to feed your dog is a high-quality commercial dog food.

So what kind of commercial food? You should feed dry food (kibble) as the staple of your Pug's diet. What's best for your Pug is a set amount of quality dry dog food, appropriate for his age and activity level, fed at the same times each day. In addition to providing complete nutrition, dry dog food also helps to scrape accumulating tartar off teeth,

cleaning teeth and keeping them strong.

When choosing a dry food choose a brand that lists some form of animal protein as its first ingredient. Make sure that somewhere on the label it indicates that the food is nutritionally complete. If you stick with a high quality brand you can be sure your Pug is getting the most digestible nutrients possible. There are standards for nutritional value in dog foods, but cheaper products may try to substitute substandard ingredients to make up their protein requirements. These poor

Once puppies are weaned from their mothers, they should be given food specially formulated for puppies until they are one year of age. These pups get their first try at solid food.

In addition to providing complete nutrition, dry dog food also helps to keep your Pug's teeth clean and strong.

Like all dogs, your Pug doesn't need variety in his diet. He will be happy eating the same thing every day.

ingredients will include animal by-products and excess grain-based ingredients. By-products include feather, hair and feet, rather than real meat. These items contain protein of some kind but are indigestible to your Pug and therefore offer no nutritional value. While your Pug needs high-quality grains as part of his diet, too many grain-based foods mean less protein. Don't skimp on the cost of the dry food; this is what your Pug will be eating day after day.

Your Pug doesn't need variety. He will be very happy eating the same thing everyday. In fact, the more consistent your Pug's diet,

the happier your dog's digestive tract will be. Pugs can easily get upset stomachs and adding leftovers or other treats to their diet can result in flatulence or diarrhea.

Many people also supplement their Pug's diet with canned food. Canned food is expensive compared to dry food. This is fine, but do not feed your dog solely canned food. If you want to offer canned food to make your Pug's food more palatable, try mixing a couple tablespoons of canned food in with the dry meal. This will give the meal added flavor without compromising its nutritional integrity.

Adult dogs instinctively need to clean their teeth, massage their gums, and exercise their jaws through chewing. There are a variety of Nylabone® toys to choose from to safely satisfy your Pug's chewing needs.

TREATS

Treats are indispensable. You will use them to help train your dog, to praise him, as a before-bed snack or simply as a little acknowledgement that you love him. It's easy to see, with all these opportunities for giving treats, that this can easily get out of hand. Your Pug never met a treat he didn't like, and too many treats could make him dangerously overweight. This is affectionate pat. This is wonderful praise that your Pug will be happy to have. Get into the habit of offering hugs and pats for work well done; this way your Pug won't come to expect treats and they will seem truly special when they do arrive. If you do offer many treats in one day, figure this into his total daily allotment and perhaps offer him less at dinner.

Carrots are rich in fiber, carbohydrates, and vitamin A. The Carrot Bone™ by Nylabone® is a durable chew containing no plastics or artificial ingredients and it can be served as-is, in a bone-hard form, or microwaved to a biscuit-like consistency.

why it's important to offer healthy treats like pieces of carrot or apple. if you like to offer dog biscuits, break off a small piece and offer that instead of the whole biscuit. Your Pug will be just as happy with a little bit; to him what's most important is that he is getting a treat from you. Also, never forget the value of an

Pugs love to eat just about anything, including things many of us would find most unsavory. A good appetite is one of the things that contributes to the Pug's eager, hearty personality, but it's up to you not to let it get out of hand. Limit your daily treat ration, feed your Pug only at mealtimes, and make sure he gets plenty of exercise.

Pugs love to eat just about anything and will always welcome a healthy treat. Be careful not to feed too many treats or your dog may become overweight.

From growing puppy to adult, your Pug will depend on you for the proper nutrition he needs.

If your Pug is healthy, happy, and clean inside and out, he is ready for the show ring.

GROOMING YOUR PUG

Grooming should be a pleasurable experience for both you and your Pug. If you train your Pug from the very beginning to accept grooming procedures, he will know what to expect and will even look forward to grooming time.

One thing that will make your grooming routine a little easier on you and your back is a grooming table. You can purchase a professional grooming table, but any waist-high table with a non-slip surface would be adequate. A professional table will have an arm to which to attach a leash or lead so the dog cannot move around as much while he is being primped. If you decide to use this device make sure you do not leave the dog in the harness unattended. And never leave your Pug on the grooming table while you answer the phone or attend to some other distracting chore. He could easily fall or leap off the grooming table, which is a dangerous distance for a small dog like your Pug.

If you train your Pug from puppyhood to accept grooming procedures, he will know what to expect and even look forward to grooming sessions.

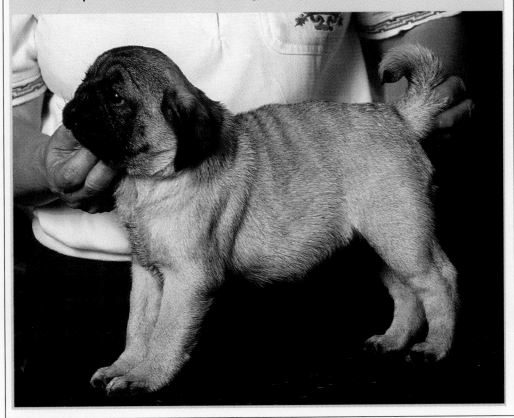

GROOMING REGIMEN

The Pug is a short-coated dog and as such does not require elaborate clipping or constant brushing to be attractive and clean. A daily brushing will suffice to remove shedding hair, though you may have to brush more frequently during certain seasons. Fawn pugs, because they have an undercoat of soft, downy hair, tend to shed more than blacks.

In addition to controlling shedding, regular brushing stimulates the dog's skin to produce the natural oils that keep the Pug's coat healthy and shiny.

It also gives you a chance to go over your Pug carefully, looking for ticks, cuts or

Your Pug's nails should be clipped on a regular basis using a good, sharp pair of guillotine-style nail clippers.

balding patches that could mean trouble. A Pug's coat is a good indicator of his overall health: A healthy Pug will have a thick, shiny, even coat. Check for hot spots (red, irritated areas where the hair is thin or missing), balding spots and excessive shedding. If you notice anything amiss, consult your veterinarian.

Finally, use the brushing routine as a chance to give your Pug a relaxing massage, and time to spend quality time with your friend helping him look and feel his best.

TOENAIL CLIPPING

A grooming chore that your Pug will probably not enjoy as much as his regular brushing is toenail clipping. For some reason, most Pugs find it extremely uncomfortable when you touch their feet. Unfortunately, it must be done. Toenails that grow too long will force the toes to splay and can eventually make walking painful to your Pug, so make sure you clip them on a regular basis.

The more you do it, the easier and quicker it will become. If you are nervous about it the first time, get your veterinarian to do it and demonstrate the procedure.

First, you must get a good, sharp pair of guillotine-style nail clippers. You will also need to have a supply of styptic powder on hand in case you cut the

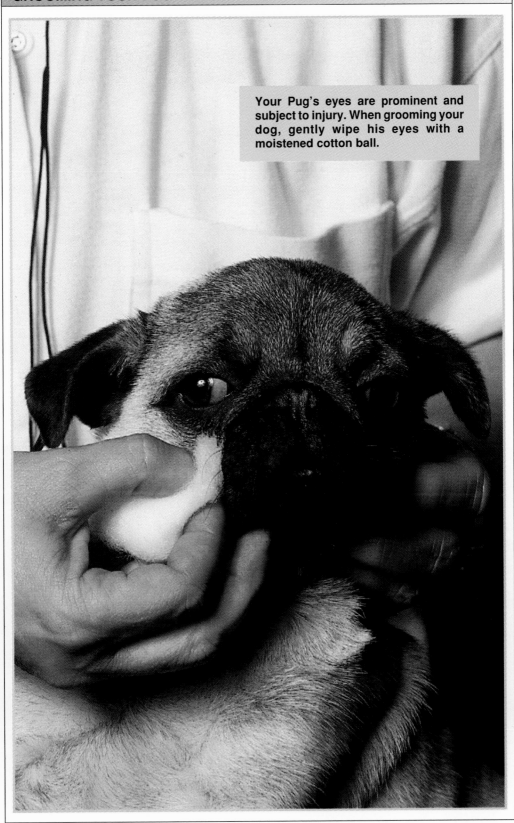

Your Pug's eyes are prominent and subject to injury. When grooming your dog, gently wipe his eyes with a moistened cotton ball.

Grooming sessions make great bonding opportunities for you and your Pug!

quick. The quick is where the blood supply to the nail ends. Hold your Pug's foot up to the light to locate the quick. If your Pug has black nails, locating the quick will be difficult and you will have to rely on your best judgment. If you can see the quick, cut the nail just above it. If recede with regular clipping and you will be less likely to catch it.

If your Pug's dewclaws (the fifth digit, equivalent to our thumbs) have not been removed, make sure you clip the nails on these as well. If they become overgrown they can grow into the animal's leg and cause a great deal of pain.

Nylafloss® serves two excellent purposes: good exercise and clean teeth. Made from 100% inert nylon products, Nylafloss® won't rot or fray like cotton tug toys.

you can't see it, cut off just a little more than the hook at the end of the nail.

If you do cut the quick accidentally, don't panic. Your Pug will be carrying on, but it's not as painful as he'd like you to believe. Apply some styptic powder and monitor the toe until the bleeding stops. The quick will

This procedure may be easier with an assistant to hold your Pug firmly while you clip the nails.

TEETH CLEANING

Good dental hygiene is as important for your Pug as it is for you. Pugs have an advantage because they don't consume all the sugar humans do, but they

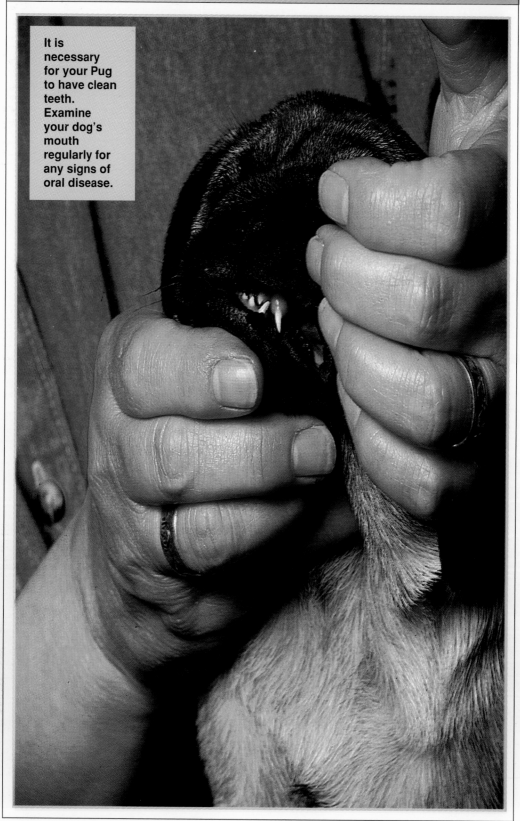

It is necessary for your Pug to have clean teeth. Examine your dog's mouth regularly for any signs of oral disease.

still need regular dental care. An easy way to help keep your dog's teeth healthy is to feed him high-quality dry dog food each day. As he chews, the dry food scrapes against the teeth, removing plaque and tartar build-up.

A yearly cleaning by your veterinarian is a good idea, but in between professional cleanings, you can keep your Pug's teeth in top shape by brushing them with a piece of gauze wrapped around the finger or a special dog toothbrush. If you choose the latter, make sure you get toothpaste made especially for dogs. Because they can't spit, toothpaste intended for humans would be swallowed by your dog and could be dangerous.

The sooner you get your Pug used to tooth care the better. As with any other procedure, a Pug who is familiar with this experience from his youngest years will be patient and tolerant.

As a pet owner, it is essential to keep your dog's teeth clean by removing surface tartar and plaque. 2-Brush™ by Nylabone® is made with two toothbrushes to clean both sides of your dog's teeth at the same time. Each brush contains a reservoir designed to apply the toothpaste, which is specially formulated for dogs, directly into the toothbrush.

Nylabones® are the only plastic dog bones made of 100% virgin nylon, specially processed to create a tough, durable, and completely safe bone.

A well-trained Pug—or group of Pugs—is a pleasure to own and will follow you wherever you go.

TRAINING YOUR PUG

You do the best to can to keep your Pug well-groomed, well fed and healthy, but you also have the teach him how to interact with the people around him for him to be truly happy and well-adjusted. In other words, you have to train him. Good training is something you committed to when you bought your Pug, just as you committed to keeping him healthy and making sure he gets plenty of exercise.

In addition, you will not be able to enjoy your Pug unless he is properly trained. A dog who does not come when he's called, who begs at the table or chases and barks at the mailman is not only a hassle, he's dangerous as well. You need to make sure your Pug comes when you call him, not just sometimes when he feels like it, but always. It could save his life in many situations. A begging Pug will not only spoil dinner for you and your family, and embarrass you in front of dinner guests, but it will also make you angry with your Pug and make him unwelcome in the house during meals. This will only make him sad and you mad, so the best

Promote constructive chewing by offering your Pug safe chew toys like Nylabones®; let him know that your personal belongings are off limits!

thing to do is train him properly from the get go. A trained Pug is a happy Pug, he knows his place in the family and how to do the right things, but most importantly, he knows how to please you and this is the most important thing for him.

There are several methods you can use to train your Pug. The most expensive is to employ a professional trainer who will whisk your Pug away and return him to you several weeks later a well-behaved pup. This certainly involves the least amount of effort on your part, but if you don't have time to spend with your dog, why do you have him in the first place? This method can be very effective for problem dogs who may need extra professional attention, but for your bright Pug puppy, it probably isn't necessary.

For his safety and the safety of others, your Pug should always wear his collar and leash during training sessions and walks.

One of the most important things about training is that it reinforces the bond between you and your dog: you are learning and succeeding together; your Pug is happy to learn because he gets happy feedback from someone he loves. This opportunity is lost with a professional trainer.

A better training strategy for your Pug puppy involves attending obedience classes. At classes you and your puppy attend together and follow the directions of a professional who is leading the class. In this way you get the best of both worlds: advice and guidance from an expert and a chance to learn with your puppy. Your puppy also has a chance to socialize with other dogs and people, an invaluable experience in his early years.

Properly socialized puppies will grow up to become properly socialized adult dogs who get along well with other dogs and humans.

To find obedience classes in your area, get in touch with the Pug Dog Club of America. They will be able to recommend a qualified instructor close to you.

Another training possibility is to "go by the book." There are many expert training books available. Using a training book can give you expertise you wouldn't have access to in your area. It can also allow you work at your own pace within your own schedule. And training with a book can be something the whole family participates in; it doesn't have to be limited to a primary caretaker. If you choose to train with a book, look for the best book you can

SUCCESSFUL DOG TRAINING is written by Michael Kamer, who trains dogs in Hollywood. It is a valuable tool in developing or enhancing your own training techniques.

EVERYONE CAN TRAIN THEIR OWN DOG, published by TFH Publications, Inc., is a reference guide arranged from A to Z that includes everything you need to know about training a dog.

buy, written by a training expert with many years of experience. Set a schedule—say a certain number of hours a week—for your training and stick to it.

Whatever way you train, make sure everyone in your household gets involved. Otherwise, your Pug may be learning one thing during his training lessons and unlearning it later at home. Make a list of the exercises your Pug is learning this week and tape them on the kitchen door so everyone in the family can help reinforce lessons.

Above all, keep training sessions short and cheerful and always end on a positive note so he remembers training sessions as fun activities rather than stressful occasions.

The proud owner of a properly trained Pug will parade him around for all to see!

A Pug being baited in the show ring. Handlers use pieces of liver or other small treats to coax their charges to behave during the judging.

SHOWING YOUR PUG

If you intend to show your Pug, you will need to start preparing long before you even acquire your dog. Start by talking to people who show dogs, especially those who show Pugs. Ask all the questions you can to learn what's involved with the dog sport. You will discover that it is a very competitive activity. Many people you will be competing against have been handling, breeding and exhibiting dogs for decades. It is a compelling activity that seems to absorb people body and soul. Don't let this intimidate you, though. These people started as novices, just like you. They were attentive and patient and learned everything they could, just as you should as you start out.

If you are still sure you want to show a Pug, you will need to acquire a dog with good show prospects. The successful show dog is very rare, one in several litters. This winning Pug closely approximates the breed standard, the official picture of the breed, in appearance and temperament. To get a Pug with show possibilities, talk to lots of breeders to learn what to look for in a show puppy.

Ch. Wolhford's Snicker Doodle owned by George W. Grimm.

When you get your puppy, the best thing to do is bring him up with the best of care, just as you would any dog. He should be playing, exercising, getting good food and plenty of love and attention from you. Start a regular grooming routine so your Pug will be used to this when the time comes to parade his good looks in the show ring.

During this stage, you need to do more preparing for your Pug's show career. First, you must memorize the breed standard. You will need to be able to recall the standard when you see Pugs in the showring. The next step is to attend dog shows. Take a close look at the dogs who are being exhibited and listen to others' critiques of them. Listen to praise as well as criticism; in fact, the praise will probably be much more helpful. If someone says "That Pug has a great front," you'll know what a good front looks like. If someone says the dog has a bad front, that doesn't really help you much. You still don't know what a good front looks like; you just know what one of many possible bad fronts looks like. Don't be so competitive that you forget you are learning.

Judge the dogs yourself against the standard. Watch carefully to see who the judges choose and try to understand why. Talking it over with other dog enthusiasts can give you an even better understanding.

Westminster Best of Breed Winner Ch. Neu's Chauncelear JB Rare, owned by Sonja Neu.

It is a good idea to attend dog shows and watch carefully as the judge examines each Pug, choosing the one that comes closest to the breed standard.

This Pug and young handler are at the World Dog Show.

This Pug is being gaited in the show ring. A Pug's gait should be free, self-assured, and jaunty.

It's also important to watch the people who lead the dogs in the show ring, the handlers. While proper handling cannot turn a bad dog into a show dog, poor handling can often obscure the attributes of a good dog and good handling can obscure the faults of a mediocre one. This will be your role in the ring: to show off your Pug to his best advantage, to make sure the judges can see him to full effect.

THE NATIONAL CLUB

A resource for you throughout the life of your Pug, especially if you will be showing him, is the Pug Dog Club of America. The national breed club can give you the name of the local Pug club in your area. From your local club, you can get the schedule of match shows in your area. Match shows are the next step to a successful showing career for you and your Pug. They differ from regular shows only in that no championship points are awarded. They are designed especially for young dogs (and new handlers) to get some experience in the ring. Match shows are the perfect opportunity for you to put to use what you have learned during all those occasions when you were just observing.

When you are finally in the ring your mind will be thinking of a hundred things at once, but try to stay focused on handling your Pug well and paying attention to the judge's next order. Don't worry about what you're up against; you will have time to see the other contestants before and after the show.

Do exactly what the judge directs. Make sure you keep clear of your Pug and the other dogs in the show ring. Most importantly, remember practice makes perfect. Enter as many match shows as you can and soon you'll start to get the hang of it. When your Pug is mature and you are confident about your handling skills, then you can move on to point shows.

It is important that your Pug is trained to stand still for long periods of time while he awaits his turn in the show ring.

YOUR PUG'S HEALTH

You are the person most responsible for your Pug's health. You will do most to ensure a healthy life for your pet by feeding him a quality diet, providing plenty of exercise to keep his system in peak condition and prevent obesity, and making sure he gets regular medical attention.

In addition to establishing a healthy routine for your Pug, make a point of getting to know your Pug's normal appearance and behavior. You know your Pug best and you will be the first to notice if anything is amiss. While you are grooming your Pug, feel for swelling or other irregularities. Watch your Pug while he runs to make sure he is moving normally. If you notice anything unusal, report it to your veterinarian immediately; your Pug's life depends on it!

The next step to keeping your Pug healthy is to find someone who can take over where you leave off: find a veterinarian whom you trust and with whom you can communicate freely. Ask friends who own dogs, preferably Pugs, what veterinarians they use, and get recommendations from your breeder or pet store. The more experience your vet has with Pugs, the better. They are a short-muzzled breed, and as such, have certain conditions best treated by someone with experience.

You must find a veterinarian who you can trust and with whom you can communicate freely. The more experience your veterinarian has with Pugs, the better.

VACCINATIONS

Your Pug will need various vaccinations to prevent lethal and dangerous diseases. The standard course of vaccinations includes protection against distemper, hepatitis, leptospirosis, parainfluenza, boirdetella, parvovirus and rabies. Your vet will advise you on the course and schedule for your Pug puppy's vaccinations, but you must make sure to stick to the schedule once it has been determined. These dis–eases are extremely dangerous, many are contagious to other animals and even to humans, and puppies are especially susceptible to them.

Distemper

Distemper is an airborne virus that affects the nervous system. Infected dogs may exhibit depression, weight loss, bloody diarrhea and eventually seizures. Hardpad, the hardening of the pads of the paws, may also occur. Even if the animal recovers, brain damage may be so severe that he will never regain control of his limbs or other body parts. Because this diseases is virtually incurable, vaccination is the best means to combat it.

Hepatitis

Hepatitis is a viral disease that affects the liver. Infected dogs will exhibit fever, abdominal pains, and convulsions. Some dogs will recover after this period of intense illness, but most infected dogs, especially puppies, succumb to the virus. Vaccination against this disease is absolutely necessary.

Leptospirosis

Leptospirosis is a bacterial disease, commonly spread by an infected dog's urine, that attacks the liver and kidneys. Symptoms include severe abdominal pain, loss of appetite and yellow eyes. Dogs can recover but a recovered dog may still be able to transmit the disease to other animals so prevention is mandatory.

Parainfluenza

This is a canine equivalent of the flu in people and is usually no more serious. Infected dogs recover, but the disease is highly contagious, often infecting entire kennels. Most boarding kennels require proof of this shot before accepting your dog. Symptoms include a dry, hacking cough and runny nose.

Your veterinarian will advise you on your Pug puppy's vaccination course and schedule, but you must make sure to stick to the schedule once it has been determined.

Parvovirus

Parvovirus was a terrible killer of puppies in recent decades. Fortunately, a vaccine has been developed, and with a good vaccination program incidence of this disease has diminished greatly. "Parvo" affects the stomach and infected dogs will experience bloody vomiting and diarrhea. The dog may have a fever and difficulty breathing. Few puppies ever recover from this deadly and painful disease so vaccination is a must!

Rabies

The best known and most feared canine disease is rabies, perhaps because it can be lethal to humans as well as dogs. Most, if not all, states require rabies vaccinations.

Rabies is often transmitted by wild animals such as raccoons and foxes. One of the first symptoms of rabies is a behavior change, making normally shy and reserved animals outgoing and aggressive. Be wary if you notice a wild animal suddenly becoming "friendly"; this is abnormal behavior and indicates something amiss. After this the animal will become increasingly antisocial, and eventually it will become comatose and die. There is no known cure for dogs, so it's easy to understand why vaccinations are a legal requirement.

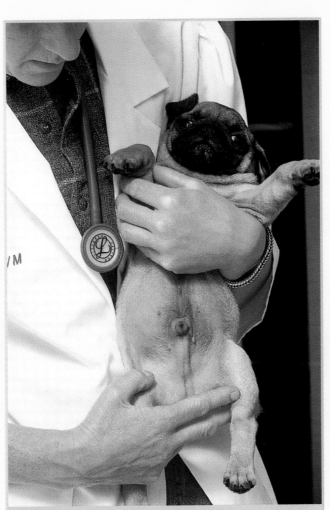

Your new Pug puppy is very vulnerable to all kinds of diseases and conditions. Your first order of business should be to take the puppy to the veterinarian.

Lyme Disease

If you live in or will be travelling in parts of the country where Lyme disease is common it's a good idea to vaccinate against this as well. Lyme disease is transmitted by deer ticks, tiny ticks that attach to the skin under the dog's coat and easily go unnoticed. Symptoms include lameness, painful and swollen joints, and fever. This disease is curable with a course of antibiotics, but it is difficult to diagnose and a dog may suffer needlessly for several months before the proper treatment is prescribed. Vaccination is preferable.

EXTERNAL PARASITES

Fleas

Fleas are probably the most common and annoying external parasite. These tiny creatures can cause a great deal of trouble. The site of their bite becomes extremely itchy and, in many dogs, flea bites cause intense allergic reactions. If you notice your dog scratching excessively or if you notice tiny black specs (flea feces) in your Pug's fur, chances are your Pug has fleas. In addition to infesting your dog, they will infest your family, home and yard if not treated quickly and effectively.

To rid your Pug of fleas, give him a flea bath. Ask your veterinarian to recommend a product and enjoy watching the fleas die a watery death in the tub. You must also wash all your Pug's bedding to make sure he is not immediately reinfested by these tiny bloodsuckers. In warmer climates, where fleas never seem to abate, it may be necessary to treat your dog with a flea spray every few days.

Ticks

Ticks are another nasty external parasite, though fortunately they tend to come one at a time. Your dog is most likely to acquire them in long grass or wooded areas, so check your Pug thoroughly when you return from an outdoor trek together. In addition to sucking your dog's blood, ticks can transmit dangerous diseases (like Lyme disease). For this reason, make sure you use a pair of tweezers rather than your bare hands when you remove the parasite.

To remove a tick, swab it with alcohol or nailpolish remover. This should make it loosen its hold on the dog, and render it easier to remove. Then, grasp the tick as close to the dog's body as possible and pull it steadily out. Wash the site of the bite with an antiseptic. If the ticks's head remains embedded in your Pug, bring him to your veterinarian to have this removed.

INTERNAL PARASITES

Internal parasites present just as much of a danger as the disease-bearing bloodsuckers mentioned above. Heartworms, tapeworms, hookworms and whipworms are all potentially dangerous to your Pug. While your adult Pug is at risk, it is worth pointing out that puppies are especially vulnerable, so do not delay or skip deworming treatments. Standard deworming of puppies starts around two weeks and continues up to three months of age. Discuss deworming procedures and worm prevention with your veterinarian.

Heartworm

Heartworm enters a dog's system by a bite from an infected mosquito. The symptoms include chronic fatigue, coughing and appetite loss. If the dog goes untreated, the worms will eventually clog the dog's heart, resulting in heart failure and death. Fortunately, heartworm is preventable with a regularly

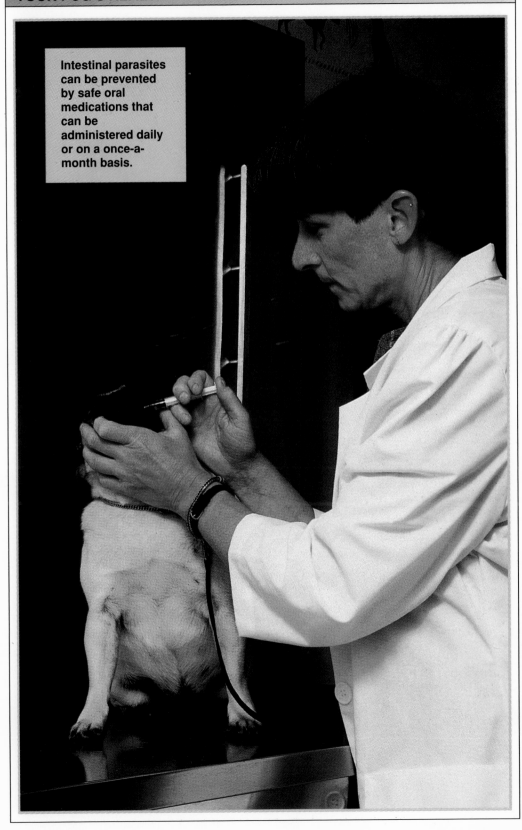

Intestinal parasites can be prevented by safe oral medications that can be administered daily or on a once-a-month basis.

administered medication available from your veterinarian. If heartworm is detected early it can be treated, but the treatment itself involves administering a form of arsenic. This is extremely dangerous for the dog, and for the older dog or puppy it can simply be too much. Consider your Pug's regular dosage of heartworm preventive as important as a vaccination, and administer it faithfully.

Roundworm

Round-worm is most commonly passed from the bitch to her litter in utero, and the standard series of puppy wormings will eliminate them. These pests can also be transmitted through infected soil and feces. People are also at risk from infection. Once inside the host, these worms will damage the liver, lungs and eventually the intestines.

It is important to be able to recognize an emergency situation and get your Pug to a veterinarian immediately.

Hookworm

Hookworm larva penetrate the skin of the dog and from there affect the lungs and windpipe, eventually making their way into the intestines where they mature. A hookworm infestation can result in intestinal damage and blood loss from the places the worms attach to the intestines. Walking your Pug in a clean exercise area will help to prevent hookworm, but a regular fecal check by your veterinarian is advisable.

Whipworm

Whipworm is transmitted through infected feces or soil. Whipworm will lodge in the intestines and cause stomach upset and diarrhea. Dogs confined to small, infrequently cleaned exercise areas are particularly susceptible. Roundworm, hookworm and whipworm are all best prevented by keeping your dog's exercise area scrupulously clean and avoiding taking your Pug to areas where many dogs congregate.

Tapeworm

Tapeworm is transmitted by fleas. Fleas carry the larvae and when the dog bites at himself to scratch the flea bite, he may swallow the flea and with it the tapeworm. Tapeworm is easily detected in the infected dog's feces, and can be treated effectively. The best approach, however, is to be diligent about flea control.

YOUR PUG'S FIRST AID

Make sure you are properly prepared for any emergency by putting together a first aid kit for your Pug. You can pack it up in a fishing tackle box or other small container for easy storage and organization. Take your first aid kit with you when you are travelling with your Pug, especially when you plan to be outdoors. You can find many of the objects in this kit in your own medicine cabinet and all are available from drug store. The important thing is that you know how to use them when the time comes.

Tweezers
Old, clean towel or absorbent rag
Hydrogen peroxide
Rectal thermometer
Antibacterial ointment
Diarrhea medicine (for humans; ask your veterinarian about dosage)
Petroleum jelly
Gauze and surgical tape
Needleless syringe

FIRST-AID EMERGENCIES

Bleeding

If your Pug cuts himself, stop the bleeding by applying pressure with a clean towel. Apply some antiseptic ointment to the wound after the bleeding stops. If the bleeding doesn't stop in a few minutes, or if the wound looks serious, get your Pug to an emergency clinic immediately.

Poisoning

Because Pugs are inclined to put everything they come across into their mouths, you must be very careful to keep dangerous substances out of reach. Keep cleaning materials in a locked cabinet (child safety locks are useful for Pug-proofing your

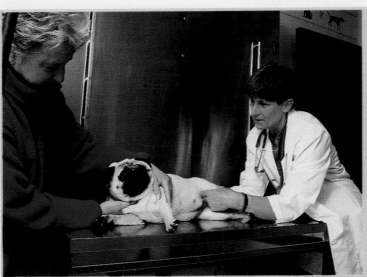

Young puppies are extremely vulnerable to internal parasites. In order to prevent infestation in your Pug, have your puppy wormed according to your veterinarian's schedule.

house). Make sure medicines are locked away, and don't place rat or mouse poisons in areas of the house to which your dog has access. One particularly dangerous substance is antifreeze, which dogs seem to find delectable. It is extremely poisonous. Make sure you keep it far out of reach of your dog, and be diligent about cleaning up any antifreeze that spills in the street or in the garage. Keep the number of your poison control center near the telephone in case of emergencies.

Symptoms of poisoning include vomiting, convulsions and salivation. If you think your Pug has been poisoned, try to figure out what it has consumed and call your poison center immediately. They will be able to advise you on the correct treatment if they know the substance that has been ingested. Do not make your dog vomit unless the poison center instructs you to do so. Some poisons can cause more trouble coming back up.

Broken Bones

If your Pug has a broken limb, get him to the vet as quickly as possible. In the meanwhile, immobilize the broken bone with several sections of newspaper rolled around the limb and fastened with tape.

Eye Injury

Because of their protruding eyes, Pugs can be more prone to eye injuries than other dogs. If your Pug injures his eye, flush it out with warm water and take the dog to the vet immediately.

Vomiting

Vomiting is usually just a result of your Pug having eaten something he shouldn't have. If it is a single episode and your dog seems otherwise healthy, don't be concerned. However if the vomiting is repeated and you notice other symptoms or unusual behavior, call your veterinarian immediately.

Diarrhea

Like vomiting, diarrhea is usually just the result of a strange addition a meal. You may want to consider offering your Pug a little diarrhea medication (ask your vet about the dosage) or just add some cooked rice to his diet. If your Pug is still experiencing diarrhea after a day or so, or if you notice any other symptoms, call your veterinarian.

Heat Stroke

Because Pugs are brachycephalic (short-nosed) they tend to overheat more easily than other breeds. Be particularly careful in the summertime; restrict exercise time to early morning and evening. Of course, you should never ever leave your Pug in the car on a hot day, even with the windows down. A car traps the heat, and the temperature in the car will rise very quickly. Although he wll certainly protest, leave your Pug at home on days like that. His life is at stake!

Symptoms of heat stroke include weakness, panting, rapid breathing, vomiting and collapse. You need to bring down your Pug's body temperature, but doing this too quickly will put the animal in shock. Apply cold compresses to the groin, neck and areas where the limbs join the body; or immerse the dog in cool, not cold, water. Call the veterinarian immediately.

POSSIBLE PUG PROBLEMS

Entropion

As a flat nosed breed, Pugs are more susceptible than many breeds to a condition called entropion in which the eyelid inverts and the eyelashes rub against the surface of the eye. This condition is painful and can lead to blindness if not addressed. The most common and successful treatment is a simple surgical procedure that raises and sutures the dog's eyelids.

Mange

There are two kinds of mange. The first, demodectic mange, is far more common in Pugs than sarcoptic mange, which is caused by a parasite and is transmittable to humans. Demodectic mange is caused by a mite and usually infests puppies. If left untreated, this will spread from a few sparse spots to a generalized bald coat. As soon as you notice a spot with thin hair or no hair at all, see the vet who will prescribe medication. Once this condition it cured, it rarely returns.

Hereditary Conditions

All breeds are prone to some inherited health conditions. Although these occur infrequently, owners should be aware of them. No dog with a hereditary health condition (or a dog who has had and has been cured of this condition) should be bred.

If your Pug is diagnosed with any of these conditions, make sure you call your breeder and let her know. Although you may not be planning to breed your Pug, the breeder should know of the existence of this disease in her line. It will be helpful when she is planning breedings in the future.

Patella Luxation

Pugs may be prone to patella luxation, in which the kneecap of or both of the hindlegs slips. As this condition progresses it can become uncomfortable and painful. Corrective surgery is usually successful.

Hemi-vertebra

This is a hereditary condition in which a vertebra fails to fuse together as the puppy is growing. It will not manifest itself until the puppy is four to eight months old. This irregular vetebra houses the nerves that control the hindquarters, and an affected puppy will be unable to control his hindlimbs, perhaps having trouble walking and later dragging the hindlimbs instead of moving them functionally. Although there is no cure for this condition, some affected dogs have benefited from a variety of treatments, including homeopathy, and are now able to live fairly normal lives.

Pug Dog Encephalitis

This is a relatively new disease, and, as little research has been done on it, it is often misdiagnosed. It involves the inflammation of the brain, and symptoms may include seizures, and head and neck pain. There is currently little that can be done to treat this condition; in fact it cannot even be firmly diagnosed until an autopsy is done. However, researchers are starting to focus more on this disease and we will probably start to see more information coming to light very soon.

YOUR OLDER PUG

An older dog is a special friend, one who knows you inside out and with whom you are supremely comfortable. Although your older Pug may not be as playful or energetic as he was when he was a youngster, he still needs the attention and affection he is used to. Adjust your routine so that you still have quality time to spend with your Pug; in his older years this time may be spent on the couch instead of frolicking in the garden. Make sure you still take your Pug for a walk around the neighborhood at least once a day. Although he may be less eager to move, he still needs the stimulation that new smells and sights provide.

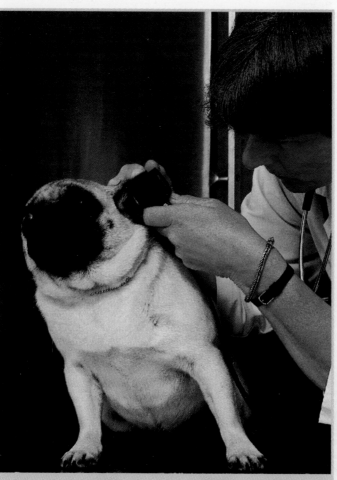

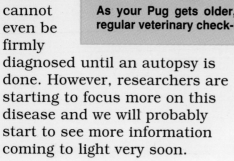
As your Pug gets older, it is imperative to maintain regular veterinary check-ups.